VLADIMIR SAVCHUK

I0533012

A BEGINNER'S
GUIDE
TO
FASTING

SIMPLE. PRACTICAL. BIBLICAL.

ISBN: 979-8-89314-030-9 paperback

ISBN: 979-8-89314-031-6 e-book

CONTENTS

1
Premise of Fasting

UNDERSTANDING FASTING

What is fasting? Why did every noteworthy person mentioned in the Bible practice fasting? Moses, David, Elijah, Esther, Daniel, Anna, and Paul are just a few people in the Bible who fasted. And of course, we know that Jesus, our Lord and Savior, fasted. In fact, He didn't start His ministry until after a 40-day fast. Moreover, when Jesus taught His disciples about fasting, He said, "*When* you fast," not "*If* you fast" (Matthew 6:16). This implies that Jesus assumed that fasting would be a normal and willingly undertaken practice for all His followers/all of us.

Fasting is voluntarily abstaining from all or some types of food and/or drink for a period of time, often as a religious observance or spiritual practice. Fasting may not be enjoyable to our flesh, but it's gratifying to know that we can exercise control over our stomach and cravings. Fasting may not be something that our flesh wants to do, but our spirit yearns for it. It can be challenging, but as we draw near to God, it brings us joy.

Fasting is temporary, not permanent. Fasting is only a temporary practice, not a permanent state. Food is a gift from God that's meant to provide us with strength, nourishment and satisfaction; it is our fuel. Without regular food intake, our bodies will not survive for very long. If we sleep eight hours a night, we are spending one third of our life asleep. For a person living 75 years, this amounts to 25 years, or 9,125 days, spent sleeping. During sleep, we are in state of fasting, which is why the morning meal is called *breakfast*—a meal you eat to break your fast. God designed our bodies to handle periods of fasting, where we pause food consumption and take a break.

Longer periods of fasting, from a few hours to a few days, and even a few weeks, are mentioned in the Bible. When we undertake anything beyond our regular sleep/overnight fast, our flesh will get irritated. But when we remember that it is only a temporary practice, we can press through.

Fasting is voluntary, not forced. Fasting shouldn't be forced on us. Just as the Holy Spirit led Jesus to fast, He will lead us. Fasting is not the same as starvation, which people experience during a famine or other circumstances. Fasting is a personal choice; starvation is forced by circumstances. It is important to always be led by the Holy Spirit when we are considering a period of fasting.

Fasting is abstaining specifically from food. When the Bible mentions fasting, it is referring to abstaining from food. In today's world, eliminating TV time, phone, or chocolate may be sacrifices or acts of self-discipline, but these things are not biblical types of fasting. Although the Bible doesn't mention abstaining from other things as forms of fasting, this also can be beneficial. This type of abstinence from other things can be an especially good practice for people who are unable to fast due to medical or other reasons.

Fasting is done for spiritual reasons. Fasting is not a diet to help you lose weight; it's a way to humble yourself before God and fervently seek Him. While there are some physical benefits to fasting, the Bible emphasizes the spiritual benefits.

Fasting is not a hunger strike. When we fast, we are not trying to manipulate and/or force God to do something. Fasting doesn't move God; instead, it moves us closer to God. It humbles us, not God. It repositions us, not God. Our main goal is to humble ourselves and to recognize our need for God.

When accompanied by prayer and sincere repentance, fasting will yield great spiritual results. Fasting is similar to prayer; it doesn't hold any power, but when we pray with fasting, we can access God's power in greater measure. Fasting increases our spiritual sensitivity and our heart's awareness of the spirit realm, where we are already seated in Christ Jesus (Ephesians 2:6-7).

Fasting in History and Other Cultures

Fasting is a practice found in all religions and cultures throughout history. Ancient Greeks practiced fasting as a form of purification before participating in religious rituals, believing it cleansed the body and mind and made them more worthy to approach the deity. Similarly, the Romans practiced fasting as preparation for certain religious ceremonies and to ward off evil influences from malevolent entities. Egyptians associated fasting with mourning and honoring the dead; they believed that it honored the gods and the dead to fast, particularly during festivals like the Feast of Thoth. The Celts viewed fasting as a way to connect with the spiritual world, gain insight, and receive visions from their gods. Even in contemporary pagan practices, fasting serves as a method of purification, spiritual preparation to receive spiritual visions and increase devotion to their gods, and as a protective measure against evil spirits.

Fasting in Judaism

In Jewish tradition and culture, fasting also plays a significant role. Historically, fasting was used to express mourning for the dead. It was a way to express submission to God, both individually and corporately. We see through their example that fasting is a way to humble ourselves before God and to seek His help. For example, Moses fasted before receiving the commandments from God. The celebration of Yom Kippur is the only fast explicitly mandated by God in the Torah, observed in the seventh month (Tishrei) as a day of atonement for the affliction and introspection of one's soul. Fasting and prayer for the atonement of sins are prescribed for all Jews, even today.

Over many centuries, rabbinic traditions and customs have introduced four additional fasting days for all Jews, beyond the Day of Atonement (Yom Kippur). These additional days of fasting were connected to the destruction of the Temple in Jerusalem. Thus, Jews now observe five days of fasting every year: one day commanded by God and four days added by the teachers of the law.

Fasting During the Time of Jesus

By the time Jesus came, a prominent Jewish sect of the Pharisees that rose to notoriety during the Second Temple period, fasted twice every week. The Gospel of Luke mentions a Pharisee who boasted, "I fast twice a week" (Luke 18:12). It was common practice for the Pharisees to fast on Mondays and Thursdays.

Jesus, who began His ministry with a 40-day fast, followed a practice similar to many others in the Bible, including Moses, who had fasted for 40 days on the mountain when he received revelation.

Jesus taught His followers that fasting should be done in secret, not accompanied by open signs of mourning or efforts to gain man's attention. Jesus' teaching on fasting focused on true humility and service to God. It directly contrasted the Pharisees' fasting. When confronted by the Pharisees about why His disciples weren't fasting the way they did, Jesus answered that once He left this earth, His disciples would fast (Matthew 9:15).

Fasting in the Early Church

The early Church precisely followed Jesus' example and teaching on fasting. Let me emphasize: They fasted *regularly*. Early Christians typically fasted twice a week, on Wednesdays and Fridays. This was documented in the Didache, an early Christian text dating from the late first or early second century. Those days were chosen to distinguish Christians from the Pharisees, who fasted on Mondays and Thursdays. Wednesday was to commemorate Jesus' betrayal by Judas, and Friday was to remember His crucifixion. They abstained from food for part of the day, typically until mid-afternoon or evening, rather than observing strict, full 24-hour fasts.

We also learn from the Didache that fasting was recommended before baptism and before taking the Lord's Supper. Early Christians fasted to strengthen their prayer life, prepare for revelation from God, express sorrow, help the poor with the food they saved, and/or to reconcile with God. Although fasting is mentioned in the Didache and other church documents, it is not taught nor commanded to believers in the writings of Paul, Peter, James, John, or Jude.

Types of Fasts

There are different types of fasts found throughout the Bible and each has unique characteristics and purposes. The Lord may lead you to more than one of these fasts at different times. Ask Him, and He will show you when and how to fast.

I. Absolute Fast

An absolute fast is sometimes referred to as a "dry fast" and refers to a fast without food or water. This fast is considered a supernatural fast. Moses went on this type of fast for 40 days (Exodus 34:28). The city of Nineveh underwent an absolute fast (Jonah 3:7), as did the Apostle Paul after his encounter with the Lord (Acts 9:9). Due to the extreme impact on the physical body, this type of fast should not be undertaken for more than three days, and should only be done if you have a clear directive from the Lord and are in good health.

2. Normal Fast

A normal fast or a "full fast" is when you don't eat any food and you only drink water. We believe that Jesus went on this type of fast for 40 days before being tempted by the devil. "And in those days, He ate nothing, and afterward, when they had ended, He was hungry" (Luke 4:2). The Bible says Jesus didn't eat anything during this time, but it doesn't mention that He did not drink anything. Usually, if a person in the Bible didn't drink anything during their fast, Scripture points that out.

3. Corporate Fast

A corporate fast is a public fast. Your private fasting should be done in secret, just as Jesus instructed in Matthew 6:16, but public fasting is fasting that is proclaimed by leaders for a group or community. We see biblical examples of this type of fasting throughout both the Old and New Testaments. The prophet

Samuel called an entire nation to a fast (1 Samuel 7:6); Esther called her Jewish people to a fast (Esther 4:16); Ezra proclaimed a fast (Ezra 8:21-23); even the pagan king of Nineveh declared a fast for his nation (Jonah 3:5); and the disciples fasted together and ministered to the Lord (Acts 13:2-3).

Along with many other pastors, I call believers to a corporate fast every January and then for a few days each month. When participating in this type of fast, it is important to examine our hearts and fast to be noticed by the Lord, not by men.

4. Daniel's Fast

Daniel's fast involves abstaining from certain foods. The Bible doesn't actually say that Daniel fasted, but the way the Bible describes his practice is commonly referred to as *Daniel's fast*. "I ate no pleasant food, no meat or wine came into my mouth, nor did I anoint myself at all, till three whole weeks were fulfilled" (Daniel 10:3). This type of fasting usually includes avoiding meat, sweets, dairy, or other pleasant foods, and focuses on fruits, vegetables, and simple foods. It is not the traditional definition of a fast, but for many believers in various circumstances, this is the most or the best they can offer to God. And God is pleased whenever we offer Him what costs us something.

5. Non-Food Fast

As I mentioned, although the biblical description of fasting (abstaining from food) does not technically apply to this type of fast, I want to highlight the non-food fast. A non-food fast is when you abstain from certain pleasant things, activities, entertainment, or gratifying pleasures other than food. This is an effective means of self-denial that is especially good for those with a medical condition. For some, the non-food fast is the safest way to practice this spiritual discipline of self-denial. Daniel didn't just avoid pleasant foods or meats, he also did not anoint himself. "I ate no pleasant food, no meat or wine came into my mouth, nor did I anoint myself at all, till three whole weeks were fulfilled" (Daniel 10:3). Paul talked about abstaining from sex for a time to give ourselves to fasting (1 Corinthians 7:5). However, it's not a mandate to abstain from sexual relations or any other specific life activities while fasting. The focus is to surrender our heart and offer our sincere dedication to God, whatever form it may take.

2

Purpose of Fasting

WHY FASTING?

Most people, even if they haven't practiced fasting, have an awareness that there are benefits to it. But why do we fast, and what are the specific benefits we can expect when we fast?

Fasting Strengthens Prayer

In the Bible, fasting is almost always connected to prayer. Jesus said, "However, this kind does not go out except by prayer and fasting" (Matthew 17:21). While God rewards the practice of fasting when it's done with the right motives, combining fasting with prayer brings the greatest results. John Wesley once said, "When you seek God with fasting added to prayer, you cannot seek His face in vain." Fasting gives a big boost to prayer. When Apostle Paul and Barnabas ordained new elders in every church, they "prayed with fasting, they commended them to the Lord in whom they had believed" (Acts 14:23). Fasting becomes that added power or intensity to prayer. Donald Whitney, in *Spiritual Disciplines*, wrote: "Fasting is one of the best friends we can introduce to prayer life."

Fasting Disconnects Us from the World

Prayer connects us to God and fasting disconnects us from the world. There are levels in God we can't reach if we are not both disconnected from the world and connected to God. Fasting, together with prayer, helps us do that. Joel 2:12 says, "Now, therefore," says the LORD, "Turn to Me with all your heart, with fasting, with weeping, and with mourning." Fasting accompanies turning to God and realigns our connection with Him.

If you want to strengthen your prayer life, add fasting to it. Fasting without prayer, while not pointless, will not yield the power that God would have us access. The purpose of fasting is to strengthen prayer. We disconnect from the world so that we can connect more deeply with God.

Fasting is the Biblical Way to Humble Ourselves

When the wicked king Ahab heard the rebuke of Elijah, he tore his clothes and put on sackcloth and fasted. God's response to Elijah was, "See how Ahab has humbled himself before Me? Because he has humbled himself before Me, I will not bring the calamity in his days. In the days of his son I will bring the calamity on his house" (1 Kings 21:29). God called Ahab's fasting humility. Indeed, we can fast but not actually humble ourselves. Fasting itself, is not humility; Ahab also tore his clothes and mourned. Fasting is your personal expression of your heart of humility before the Lord.

David similarly mentioned fasting as a way to humility: "I humbled myself with fasting" (Psalm 35:13). Ezra had the same reference to fasting and humility. "Then I proclaimed a fast there at the river of Ahava, that we might humble ourselves before our God…" (Ezra 8:21). The Bible gives us a command to humble ourselves before God. We shouldn't pray for God to humble us, nor should we wait for life to humble us. We choose to humble ourselves by giving serious attention to Almighty God, taking ourselves off the throne through fasting.

When fasting is used to humble ourselves before God, it can't escape God's attention. The choice is ours. The Bible emphasizes the importance of humility: God teaches the humble (Psalm 25:9), lifts up the humble (Psalm 147:6), gives grace to the humble (Proverbs 3:34), and gives wisdom to the humble (Proverbs 11:2). Honor and life and riches come by humility (Proverbs 22:4), God dwells with humble people (Isaiah 57:15), and the humble are great in God's kingdom (Matthew 18:4). This doesn't mean that if we just fast, all these promises automatically become ours. Fasting must be a personal expression of humility. It's humility that God is looking for, and fasting is a good friend of prayer and humility.

Fasting as an Expression of Grief

In the Bible, three or four references to fasting mention it as an expression of grief. Fasting was a common practice when someone faced great anxiety, loss, or grief. It wasn't only to seek God's solution in times of hardship, but also a way of dealing with sorrow. The men of Jabesh Gilead fasted for seven days to mourn King Saul's burial (1 Samuel 31:13). David did the same—he mourned and fasted until evening for Saul and his sons (2 Samuel 1:12). Later on, David fasted at Abner's death (2 Samuel 3:31-39). Nehemiah mourned, fasted, and prayed when he heard about the state of Jerusalem (Nehemiah 1:4), and the book of Daniel tells us that King Darius fasted while Daniel was in the lion's den (Daniel 6:18).

Fasting and mourning are often mentioned together (Joel 2:12-13). It's normal and at times necessary to weep, mourn, grieve, and lament. The largest category in the book of Psalms is laments. David was familiar with these emotions. And there is an entire book in the Bible named Lamentations. Jesus promised us comfort in mourning when He said, "Blessed are those who mourn, for they shall be comforted" (Matthew 5:4). Fasting provides a healthy way to process sadness and seek this comfort from God.

Fasting to Seek God's Deliverance

The most common fast in the Bible was to seek God's salvation from enemies. Ezra fasted when faced with danger on the way to Jerusalem, asking God for divine protection (Ezra 8:21-28). Esther fasted when she faced evil Haman and realized there was no other way or hope for the Jews (Esther 4:16). Jehoshaphat fasted when the Canaanite and Syrian armies were invading (2 Chronicles 20:3). According to psychology, the two basic human responses to danger are fight or flight. But God offers us a third response: fasting.

That's what Jehoshaphat did as king—he sought the Lord through fasting, rather than immediately fighting or fleeing. Fasting gets us back in touch with the almighty God, who is able to deliver us.

Sometimes we face problems bigger than ourselves, but they are not bigger than God. History is full of godly people who learned to face life's calamities on their knees with fasting. What the enemy meant for evil, God turned for their good. This same God is our God today. Whatever the enemy means for evil in our lives, God will turn for our good if we seek to follow and be faithful to Him. In many instances, fasting turns into feasting. God turns mourning into joy, sickness into healing, defeat into victory. It's not that fasting has its own power, but fasting exposes our powerlessness. Then, in our weakness, we find God to be our strength and source of refuge.

When you hit rock bottom, get on your knees, humble yourself before God, and fast. You will discover God to be not only God of the mountains but also God of the valleys. If life has broken you down, break your pride and fast. You will find God bringing your breakthrough on the other side. Trust Him!

Fasting to Restore Our Hunger for God

We often only think of physical hunger when we think of fasting, but fasting renews our spiritual hunger and connection to God. It's interesting how this works: Physical hunger done with the goal of seeking Jesus makes our spiritual hunger for Him even stronger. Fasting brings a fresh fire of zeal and passion for Him. Jesus indicated that His disciples would fast when He was gone (Mark 2:20). Fasting is that longing of the Bride (the Church) for the Bridegroom. It's physical pain that stirs spiritual craving for the Lord.

Fasting not only rekindles our hunger for God, but it also serves as a way to minister to the Lord. In Luke 2:37, Anna, an 84-year-old widow, didn't depart from the temple but "served God with fastings and prayers night and day." Fasting accompanied by prayer is one way we can serve the Lord. As a pastor and minister of the Lord, Anna's example is a vital reminder that I must not only minister to people, but also minister to the Lord through fasting and prayer. Every minister of the Lord must learn to minister to the Lord like she did. That's where the secret lies. Similarly, Acts 13:2 tells us that Saul and Barnabas "… ministered to the Lord and fasted…" Serving or ministering to the Lord is done best through worship and prayer accompanied with fasting. Just as Paul's missionary calling was birthed during a season of ministering to the Lord, our own ministries are strengthened and directed when we engage in prayer and fasting.

Fasting to Prepare Us for God's Calling

Many see fasting as a response to crisis or a solution for problems, but it's more than that. Fasting is also a preparation to fulfill God's calling. Before Nehemiah reinforced the gaps and rebuilt the wall around Jerusalem in 52 days and before he gathered his people together, equipping them to rebuild the city walls, he fasted. Nehemiah 1:4 says, "So it was, when I heard these words, that I sat down and wept, and mourned for many days; I was fasting and praying before the God of heaven." A season of weeping and prayer with fasting paved the way for him to fulfill God's purpose for his life.

Fasting should not be reserved for crisis and problems, but also to seek our calling. Jesus' fasting in the wilderness occurred before the start of His ministry. It was after a season of fasting and testing that Jesus returned "in the power of the Holy Spirit" to fulfill His assignment (Luke 4:14). As I mentioned, Paul and Barnabas fasted and ministered to the Lord before they were launched into missionary work. Later in their missionary journey, Paul and Barnabas appointed elders for churches by committing them to the Lord with prayer and fasting. That was how God launched them into their ministry, and then they followed this same pattern to launch other elders into their assignment, establishing a pattern for ministry that included fasting and prayer. Reflecting on their example, I wonder how much our service to God would change if we brought fasting with prayer back into the core practices of our ministry.

When Jesus' disciples tried to drive a demon out of a boy, Jesus attributed their failure to unbelief. Although Jesus ordained them to cast out demons, the solution to this failed attempt was fasting mixed with prayer. He said, "However, this kind does not go out except by prayer and fasting" (Matthew 17:21). This doesn't mean that every time we minister deliverance, we have to fast, but we must make prayer and fasting a regular spiritual practice in our life if we want to be effective in our ministry to God. The lack of prayer and fasting will result in the lack of power in ministry. No prayer with fasting will bring about no power in ministry.

Fasting as Preparation for Temptation

When we are facing trials and temptation, our human effort will never give us sustained victory; we need the power of God. In order to access more of God's power, fasting can be done both in a time of trial and as a preparation for trial and temptation. Adam's first temptation, Israel's trials after their exodus from Egypt, and Jesus' own temptation in the wilderness were all related to food. Fasting addresses our natural cravings and puts them on the cross, and helps us to present our body as a living sacrifice to God. Our body is meant to be our servant, not our master. If we are not careful, our flesh can easily dominate and become our master. If that happens, what Paul said to the Philippians will describe us: We will be people "whose end is destruction, whose god is their belly, and whose glory is their shame—who set their minds on earthly things" (Philippians 3:19).

I am not saying that if we don't fast, our stomach becomes our god, but fasting does help to dethrone "king belly" off its highly exalted throne. When our body's appetites are submitted to the Holy Spirit, it's easier to set our minds on heavenly things. Fasting disciplines our flesh to know it doesn't get what it wants or craves. It shows our soul and flesh who the boss is in your life. Then, when tough temptations come, it's easier to resist the flesh's urges because the flesh has already been trained to submit to the Spirit. Fasting helps us to get control of our appetites.

Additionally, the discipline of fasting has a domino effect on other spiritual disciplines. It develops more godly willpower, more dedication, more motivation, and more passion for God. If you struggle with self-discipline, add fasting to your prayer. Jesus promised us that if we seek the Kingdom of God, He will cause other things to be added to us (Matthew 6:33). When you commit to prayer and fasting, you will notice how other areas of your life, where you lacked control or dominion, will begin to come into alignment.

Fasting and Healthy Relationship with Food

As fallen human beings, we are experts at turning good things into gods. Food is one of these good things that we often worship. Has the fridge become your friend? Has alcohol become your ally? In our culture, we don't hide the fact that we use food as counterfeit comfort; we call these foods "comfort foods." Fasting is a powerful way to expose our unhealthy relationship with food. We know that food is a gift from God. We have food on earth, and we will have food in heaven. If we're not careful, here on earth we can get so enchanted with flavors and good smells that food becomes an idol to us. Instead of living a crucified life that leads to resurrection, we end up living a carnal life that leads to ruin. Food stops being our fuel; it becomes our friend, and that should not be! Please hear me: Food is not your friend; it's meant to nourish the cells of your body.

During hard times, we should seek comfort from the Holy Spirit, not derive it from food. Fasting exposes these toxic feelings or attitudes so that we choose to find real comfort in God, not in food.

3

Process of Fasting

Consult with your doctor.

Fasting is not for everyone. If you're pregnant or nursing, it may be dangerous to fast. If you're on medication, taking any prescription or over-the-counter medications to treat pre-existing conditions, it's crucial to check with your doctor first. Fasting can be dangerous in these situations and may not be a good option for you. Also, if you have some sort of event coming up that will demand a lot of physical energy, fasting can be challenging and affect your performance. In these cases, I encourage you to consider a type of non-food fast that I mentioned earlier.

Avoid fasting if you're under 18.

Don't fast if you're under 18 years old. Minors are discouraged from fasting food and should never engage in fasting without express parental consent and oversight. Minors who desire to fast are also encouraged to consider non-food abstentions, such as TV, movies, internet surfing, video games and other entertainment. If older teenagers choose to fast from food under their parents' supervision, we encourage them to use juice and protein drinks to support their health, growth and metabolism.

Set a goal.

Determine the purpose for your fast. No matter what type of fast you begin, you must have a goal. Define your reason for not eating. Be specific about it. Write it down in your journal to remind you. Do you need direction in life's decisions, healing, restoration of your marriage, family issues, or wisdom? Are you facing financial difficulties? Ask the Holy Spirit for guidance and present your goals to God in prayer.

Choose type and length of the fast.

The type of fasting you select is up to you and the Lord. You could go on a full fast, where you don't eat, but only drink liquids. You may desire to forego sweets and meats like Daniel, and only eat vegetables and drink water. Pay attention to what the Holy Spirit leads you to do and then endeavor to do it. Stick to it. Also decide how long you will fast. Remember, you may fast as long as you like, as the Lord leads. And be courteous enough to inform whoever prepares your meals about your plans to fast. Most people can easily fast from one to three days, but you may feel God's grace and leading to go longer, even as long as 21 to 40 days. Use wisdom and pray for guidance. Beginners are advised to start slowly.

Cut back on solid foods and caffeine.

Avoid overeating before you start fasting.
Stuffing yourself before fasting shows that your
heart is in the wrong place and food is overly
important to you. The best thing to do is to cut
back on heavy food the night before or even
a day before. Also, cut back on caffeine days
before fasting in order to avoid headaches.

Replace eating with time with God.

Fasting is not the time to get more work done;
it's time to devote to God. Fasting is as much
about not eating physical food as it is about
feeding on spiritual food. Spend time listening
to praise and worship music. Read and med-
itate on the Bible throughout the day. Let the
hunger pangs remind you to stop everything
and pray. Pray as often as you can during the
day. Get away from normal distractions as
much as possible, and keep your heart and
mind set on seeking God's face. Fill your free
time with reading, praying and journaling.
Remove entertainment! Fasting is a spiritual
detox. Think of fasting as a time of feasting

on God's Word in His presence. The Word of God is spiritual food for a spiritual person. That's why during His time of fasting, Jesus told the devil, "Man shall not live by bread alone, but by every word that proceeds from the mouth of God" (Matthew 4:4).

Expect initial challenges.

The first 72 hours are the hardest. Your body's glucose (sugar) level drops during the first few days of fasting. Glycogen, which is stored in the liver, is converted to glucose and then released into the blood to restore your blood to the average glucose level. It is recommended to get as much rest as you need. Your weight will go down in the first days of the fast, due to a considerable amount of water exiting the body. Your body will eliminate excess water, which may result in frequent urination. This can happen even if you don't drink much water, because insulin holds onto water. When your body stops producing insulin during your fast, that excess water leaves your body.

Drink water, but not too much.

You will likely drink more water during your fast but be careful not to drink too much. If you drink like a camel, trying to store water, you will wash out all the nutrients and minerals in your body. Instead, add low-calorie electrolytes or mineral salt to your water. Some prefer to drink coconut water instead of regular water. It is also wise to abstain from strong stimulants such as caffeinated and sugary drinks during a fast, including artificial sweeteners found in diet drinks. You will want to avoid soy protein drinks, which have been known to cause health problems during a fast.

Manage hunger and side effects.

When you fast, your body eliminates toxins from your system. This is called detoxification. When it happens, it can cause mild discomfort such as headaches and irritability during withdrawal from caffeine, sugars and carbs. And naturally, you will have hunger pangs. Avoiding water can make you feel even hungrier, since water helps increase satiety. If you don't eat food or drink water, your body begins to crave fuel. You'll likely feel fatigued, dizzy, and weak. David said of his fasting: "My knees are weak through fasting, and my flesh is feeble from lack of fatness" (Psalms 109:24).

You may also feel more irritable when you fast. As the hunger builds up, you're bound to feel cranky. Therefore, mood swings are pretty common. And, when you're tired and hungry, it can be difficult to concentrate at school or work.

Maintain regular hygiene.

Jesus said that when we are fasting, we should wash our face. He was referring to the cultural practice where fasting was a part of mourning for the dead along with a public display of sorrow and grief. Ripping clothes, putting ashes on one's head and not washing were a part of that ritual. However, when you're fasting, it's important to shower and brush your teeth often. Metabolism starts to convert fat cells to fatty acid, so your fat starts melting and the broken-down fat is expelled through exhaling. Yes, it is interesting that fat does not go out through urine, poop, or sweat; it exits the body through breathing.

Limit physical activity.

Opt for light exercise like walking, which is the most practical and ancient form of exercise. Your body's go-to supply of fuel (sugar) will run out within a day or two of fasting. At this point, and *only at this point*, your body proceeds to its backup fuel source: fat. Fat is something we all have enough of (unless you're an Olympic marathon runner or Mr. Olympia). The average human has 34 pounds of fat. That's 68 days' worth of fuel for your body to feed on. This means that when you fast, not only is your body not starving itself, but you've opened the doors to an internal all-you-can-eat buffet of fat. If you're only fasting one day, then there is no problem with normal exercising, but if you're going for longer than two days, you might be too tired to do normal activity, which is okay. Take time to be with God and reduce your exercise to something minor like taking a prayer walk.

Reintroduce food gradually.

When you are ready to end your fast, make a firm decision to end it slowly. This time period, of course, depends on the length and the type of fast. If it was only a one-day fast, usually there is no harm in resuming normal eating. If you go for more than three days, you must begin eating solid food very gradually (see below for suggestions). Start by eating soups or small portions that are easy to digest. Eating solid foods too soon and/or overeating is extremely dangerous to your digestive system.

The longer you fast, the longer it takes your body to come out of a time of abstinence. When coming back from a fast of 10 days or more, the break-in period should be extended one day for every four days of fasting. The 21-day fast should take at least 3 days to return to normal eating. The 40-day fast should take at least seven days to resume eating your normal diet. The rule is that you should never break the fast (longer than 2 days) by eating a normal meal. During a fast, the stomach has been slowly shrinking. By the end of the fast, the stomach's capacity for handling food is nothing like it was at the beginning. The organs in the body that are normally assimilating food have taken a rest. They have gone into a "deep sleep." The longer the fast, the deeper the sleep. Most body processes dial down when you don't eat for a long while. The body needs to produce enzymes that are capable of breaking food down once again, ramp up bile production, and have enough acid to break foods down in the stomach.

If you start eating too much food right after a fast, it results in stomach cramps, bloating, nausea, stomach pain, and diarrhea. It pretty much nullifies the physical benefits of fasting. In some cases, it can even cause serious irreversible complications with the digestive system. Eating normally too soon after prolonged fasting has even caused physical death for some people. You should never come out of a long fast with a normal meal that includes animal proteins, bread, sugar, dairy, or processed foods.

Exiting a fast correctly demands at least as much discipline as fasting itself. I think it requires even more discipline to exit fasting correctly than not to eat during a fast. To avoid digestive issues, coat your stomach by drinking water from cooked rice or water-based broths. Soft, sweet fruits like melon, watermelon, papaya, and mango are good to eat, following the water-based broths. Eat very small portions of bone broth, cooked tomato, or steamed vegetables. You can add tofu to some broccoli, which will help to add substance.

4

Pitfalls of Fasting

WHAT NOT TO DO WHEN YOU'RE FASTING

Fasting as a Political Tool

Not every fast aligns with biblical principles. For instance, using a fast as a political weapon might have some positive results, but it's not a biblical fast. Jatin Das, while on trial, fasted for 116 days to improve conditions in prisons in India. He died, but his response sparked reforms. Mahatma Gandhi undertook prolonged fasts over 18 times during his life. His hunger strike in 1932 led to the Poona Pact, under which the leaders of the untouchable caste renounced separate representation during British rule. Fasting as a political strategy is no more than a hunger strike; it's a means to enforce change in the world. But that's not the fast that God rewards. A biblical fast is directed toward God, not the government. A biblical fast brings change within us; it doesn't demand change in those around us.

Fasting as a Modern Trend for Better Health.

Intermittent fasting has become popular for health and fitness. Its focus is on losing weight, improving health, and simplifying life. It has powerful effects on your body and brain and may even help you live longer. Intermittent fasting is a 16 to 24-hour fast by skipping breakfast, and possibly other meals. While I appreciate all the benefits associated with doing intermittent fasting, and I practice it most of the time, biblical fasting is different than intermittent fasting. The focus of a biblical fast is on spiritual health. While we may reap physical benefits of fasting, its main purpose must be spiritual. Remember the definition of fasting: It's a voluntary absence of food for spiritual reasons. Losing weight might be a benefit of fasting, but it's never the purpose. Moreover, almost everyone I know who had lost weight during fasting soon gained it back. Fasting is the worst way to lose weight because weight loss requires a change of lifestyle, not simply going without food for an extended period of time.

Fasting as a Sacrifice While Avoiding a Life of Obedience.

The elders of Jezreel, under the influence of Jezebel, fasted to condemn Naboth, an innocent man. Their fast was rooted in blatant disobedience to God. They were condemning an innocent man to death and their fasting was entirely displeasing to God (1 Kings 21:11-13).

Do you remember your school days when you were allowed to bring in an extra-point assignment in addition to your homework? Fasting, along with humble obedience to God's moral standard, is like getting extra points added to your homework. But if you don't live a life that's obedient to God, using a fast to compensate for the lack of obedience will not do anything for you. It's like when King Saul tried to bring God a sacrifice but was disobedient at the same time. His sacrifice didn't matter at all to God (1 Samuel 15:22). If you're living in a known sin, hoping that fasting will put all of that under the rug and get you a favor with God, it doesn't work!

Forced Fasting by those in Authority.

Again, fasting should be voluntary, not forced. King Saul, in an attempt to defeat an advancing enemy army, forced his men to fast in the midst of battle. That was a foolish and selfish act. Saul ignored the timing—the men needed to eat during war to have strength and nourish their bodies. He decided he could take vengeance on his enemies and defeat them if his soldiers fasted. It had nothing to do with God and everything to do with Saul's personal vengeance. God was not in that fast. That fast was enforced by fear. Moreover, Saul cursed anyone who wouldn't fast. Biblical fasting is voluntary, not compulsory. There are blessings in a biblical fast, with no curse attached to not fasting. After those men finished this foolish fast, they ended up eating food with blood— something God's law prohibited. This fast was enforced by a man, not by the Spirit of God; it was led by fear, not by faith; it led to sin, not to the greater righteousness of God.

Be careful of those who make people fast; that's not biblical. Be wary of those who curse or condemn those who don't fast; that's what Saul did. It's wrong, and it's not biblical. As a side note, Jesus defended His disciples in front of the Pharisees when they were criticized for not fasting. He didn't curse them; He defended them. But He also said that the day would come when they would fast (Matthew 9:14-15).

Fasting that Ignores the Poor.

The fast that ignores people in need is the fast that God will ignore. The fast that ignores God is the fast that God will ignore. Isaiah 58 condemns wrongful conduct during a fast. "'Why have we fasted,' they say, 'and You have not seen? Why have we afflicted our souls, and You take no notice?' In fact, in the day of your fast you find pleasure, and exploit all your laborers" (v. 3). How did they ignore God while fasting? While fasting, they also oppressed others (v. 6). While fasting, they ignored those in need (v. 7). While fasting, they also pointed fingers at others and spoke wickedness (v. 9). The fast that ignores the poor, also ignores God. Fasting that ignores helping others when it's in our power to do so, also ignores God. Fasting that tolerates the verbal diarrhea of wickedness, gossip, and lies, is the fast that God will ignore. The fast God chooses includes sharing your bread with the hungry, loosing the bonds of wickedness, and treating others with kindness and respect.

Fasting to Impress Others

Lastly, it's wrong to fast to impress others! Jesus addressed this in His Sermon on the Mount, when He warned against fasting for show. I find it interesting that Jesus didn't judge people who didn't fast; instead, He corrected those who fasted for the wrong reasons. He called them hypocrites. The word *hypocrite* has its origin in acting on a stage.[1] In acting, an actor performs a role for the audience, but that role is not their true nature. An actor is pretending to be someone they are not. Jesus warned us that it's possible to put on a false display of virtue through fasting. Fasting that's done to show off how spiritual or how disciplined we are, misses heaven. God is not going to punish us for that kind of fast; He just will not reward us for it. The reward for this kind of fast comes from men. Because it is only an act, we are really doing it to be recognized by others.

People who want others to view them as spiritual because of fasting have to keep in mind that most other people simply don't care that they are fasting! Therefore, it's best to keep our fasting secret to God, to please Him with our sacrifice, and not to garner applause from men. Fasting is not a performance for men; it's humbling ourselves before God. We are not on a stage acting before men, we are

---

1 Hypocrite: What's the Origin of Hypocrite?" Merriam-Webster, www.merriam-webster.com/wordplay/hypocrite-meaning-origin

sincerely pursuing God in our heart, seeking *His* recognition and *His* reward.

So, when you fast, keep your fast private and don't blow a trumpet. If you do tell someone that you're fasting, make sure it's out of necessity, not out of fishing for a compliment. Don't draw attention to yourself or to your fasting. Go about your normal day and don't make a big deal about fasting. Don't try too hard to hide your fasting, nor hype it up. God wants to reward you for fasting, not punish you for not fasting. The focus of your fasting is not on the fast itself, but on the Father. Fast unto Him.

In conclusion, fasting should be a sincere, spiritual practice aimed at drawing closer to God, not a tool for political agendas, health trends, or social status. Approach fasting with the right heart, focusing on spiritual growth and compassion, and let your fasting be a genuine expression of your desire for a deeper relationship with God.

5

Power of Fasting

Public reward.

In His teaching on fasting, Jesus promised that when fasting is done with pure motives, it brings public reward. "So that you do not appear to men to be fasting, but to your Father who is in the secret place; and your Father who sees in secret will reward you openly" (Matthew 6:18). Fasting, like prayer and giving, is a private discipline that yields public benefits. The Father not only sees your fasting, but also rewards it. While the Bible doesn't specifically tell us what that reward is, two things are clear: It's God who brings about that reward, not men; and that reward will be open—others will see it. While the public reward is not the motive for fasting, those who do fast in secret will reap an open reward.

Favor to Those Who Fast.

Though the Bible doesn't clearly state that God gives favor to those who fast, it's evident that fasting accompanies humility, and God gives grace to those who are humble (Psalm 35:13; 1 Peter 5:5). Grace is undeserved favor, and we know that favor is not fair. Perhaps, this favor is a part of God's open reward. How this favor manifests in the life of a believer will be different for everyone.

Stronger Spiritual Life.

A guaranteed reward of biblical fasting is a stronger spiritual life! A person's prayer life will be stronger. Sensitivity to the Holy Spirit will be stronger. Fire for God will become stronger. Hunger for God's Word will be greater. Fasting brings fresh fire, and the cravings of the flesh will be subdued. Spiritual disciplines are God's methods to make us more like Him. The result of fasting is that we become more like Jesus, which is the essence of true biblical spirituality.

God gives the following promise to people who embrace true fasting:

"Then your light shall break forth like the morning, your healing shall spring forth speedily, and your righteousness shall go before you; the glory of the LORD shall be your rear guard. Then you shall call, and the LORD will answer; You shall cry, and He will say, 'Here I am'" (Isaiah 58:8-9).

1. ***Your light will break forth like the morning***. There will be a dawn of a new day in your spiritual life, ending a season of confusion and darkness.

2. ***Your healing will spring forth speedily.*** God promises healing to those who fast. Later in this chapter, God promises to "strengthen your bones" (Isaiah 58:11). That means He gives you renewed strength.

Studies confirm that fasting promotes blood sugar control by reducing insulin resistance. It helps to lower inflammation and increases a growth hormone vital for metabolism. Thus, fasting is a physical detox for the body. As toxins are removed, healing springs forth.

3. **Your righteousness will go before you.** You don't become righteous through fasting, because righteousness is a gift of God through Jesus. Walking in righteousness requires you to work out what God has worked within. That's where spiritual disciplines come in. One personal discipline leads to strength in another. As you begin to practice fasting, you will be led to develop other spiritual disciplines that lead to righteous living.

4. **The glory of God will be your rear guard.** Just as God went ahead of Israel in a pillar of cloud by day and a pillar of fire by night, His glory also

becomes your guard. Righteousness goes before you with God's glory coming behind you. Goodness and mercy follow you all the days of your life (Psalm 23:6).

5. *The Lord will answer your cry.*
Fasting strengthens prayer. Fasting accompanied by fervent prayer brings about answers.

"The LORD will guide you continually, and satisfy your soul in drought, and strengthen your bones; you shall be like a watered garden, and like a spring of water, whose waters do not fail. Those from among you shall build the old waste places; you shall raise up the foundations of many generations; and you shall be called the Repairer of the Breach, the Restorer of Streets to Dwell In" (Isaiah 58:11-12).

1. *The Lord will guide you continually.*
God will order your footsteps and establish your path. He will lead you in the way of righteousness for His name's sake.

2. ***The Lord will satisfy your soul in a dry place.*** You will flourish in drought because your roots are deep in the Lord. You will be fruitful in times of famine. Even in hard times, God will show His power. He will feed you, even in parched regions. God doesn't change your circumstances to provide for you; He will take care of you even in difficult places.

3. ***You will be like a watered garden, a spring of water, whose waters do not fail.*** You will be a blessing to others. Gardens bless others. God will bless you to become a blessing to others.

4. ***You will rebuild the city's ruins.*** God will use you to rebuild what the enemy has destroyed. You will re-establish the ancient foundations and become a rebuilder of walls. God wants to use you to redig ancient wells of revival.

5. ***You shall be called the repairer and the restorer.*** You will become known as the rebuilder of walls and

restorer of homes. God will give you influence that is connected to the dynamic impact that you will make in His kingdom.

When you make fasting part of your life, you will find these and many more promises to be true for you. God is always faithful to His Word—when you seek the Lord with fasting, you will find Him!

Thank you for reading!

I hope that this short booklet has brought clarity on fasting, and most importantly, that it has lit some fire in your heart to fast. For more insights on fasting, check out my YouTube video teachings and audio podcast content on the topic. Additionally, you and your small group can take my free e-course on fasting, as well as my 21-day devotional, *Fast Forward*, where I share a lot of my personal stories about fasting and teach you how you can fast effectively for 21 days.

Happy fasting!

Thank You for Reading

We hope this book was a blessing to you. To help you dive deeper, we also offer a study guide and e-course videos to accompany it. These resources are great for weekly small-group discussions!

We also offer reading plans on the YouVersion Bible App to enhance your study and integrate God's Word into your daily life.

If this book was a blessing to you, would you also consider leaving a review on Amazon or Goodreads and sharing it on your social media? This will go a long way in helping others discover this book and grow in their walk with God.

For more information and access to all our resources, please visit pastorvlad.org.

Partner with Us

Vladimir Savchuk Ministries offers a number of biblical resources such as courses, videos, reading plans, and books that have been translated into more than a dozen languages, all free of charge. We are also involved in humanitarian aid around the world, helping those in need.

Our desire is that people from every nation would be able to learn about Jesus Christ and grow in their walk with God. Would you consider offering a one-time gift or becoming a partner to help us continue providing these free resources to people around the globe?

We believe that everyone should have access to free biblical content, and your donations and support help make it possible.

To learn more about our ministry's vision and impact, or to donate, please visit www.pastorvlad.org/donate.

Other Books

Break Free

How to Get Free and Stay Free

Single, Ready to Mingle

God's Principles for Relating, Dating, and Mating

Fight Back

Moving from Deliverance to Dominion

Fast Forward

Accelerate Your Spiritual Life Through Fasting

Host the Holy Ghost

Build Fire

How to overcome storms, setbacks, and spiritual attacks

Available everywhere books are sold in paperback, electronic, audio version.

You can also download a free PDF on www.pastorvlad.org/books

Stay Connected

www.pastorvlad.org

www.vladschool.com

www.facebook.com/vladhungrygen

www.x.com/vladhungrygen

www.instagram.com/vladhungrygen

www.youtube.com/vladimirsavchuk

If you have a testimony from reading this book, let us know:
www.pastorvlad.org/testimony
If you wish to post about this e-book on your social media, please use tag @vladhungrygen and use #pastorvlad hashtag.

www.ingramcontent.com/pod-product-compliance
Lightning Source LLC
Chambersburg PA
CBHW071543120626
46550CB00006B/2557